10 CLASSICS IN 10 MINUTES

10 CLASSICS IN 10 MINUTES

The World's Fastest-Talking Man Teaches the World's Greatest Lessons

Conceived and Written by Andy Mayer and Jim Becker

Performed by John "Mighty Mouth" Moschitta

Illustrations by Mark Brewer

BARNES & NOBLE BOOKS

NEW YORK

This edition published by Barnes & Noble, Inc., by arrangement with becker&mayer!
2004 Barnes & Noble Books
M 10 9 8 7 6 5 4 3 2 1

Editorial: Conor Risch
Design: Todd Bates
Production coordination: Leah Finger
Project management: Sheila Kamuda

ISBN 0-7607-5556-6

Library of Congress Cataloging-in-Publication data is available.

Printed in Malaysia

10 CLASSICS IN 10 MINUTES

The World's Fastest-Talking Man Teaches the World's Greatest Lessons

Conceived and Written by Andy Mayer and Jim Becker

Performed by John "Mighty Mouth" Moschitta

Illustrations by Mark Brewer

BARNES & NOBLE BOOKS

NEW YORK

This edition published by Barnes & Noble, Inc., by arrangement with becker&mayer!
2004 Barnes & Noble Books
M 10 9 8 7 6 5 4 3 2 1

Editorial: Conor Risch
Design: Todd Bates
Production coordination: Leah Finger
Project management: Sheila Kamuda

ISBN 0-7607-5556-6

Library of Congress Cataloging-in-Publication data is available.

Printed in Malaysia

CONTENTS

MOBY DICK

MOBY DICK is a true American classic. Herman Melville's rich, textured prose captures the romance of the sea as well as the camaraderie of the human spirit. MOBY DICK is much more than the story of a whale; it is a treatise on man's place in the universe. Here now is MOBY DICK in exactly one minute.

Call me **ISHMAEL**. And so our great adventure begins. Ishmael has time to kill. He's bored. He's broke. How about a trip to sea? Why not? First off: New Bedford. The weather's crummy. He's beaten. All the inns are booked solid, so he shares a room with a harpoon-hurtling heathen named **QUEEQUEG**. Now they're the best of friends. They decide to ship out together, but first

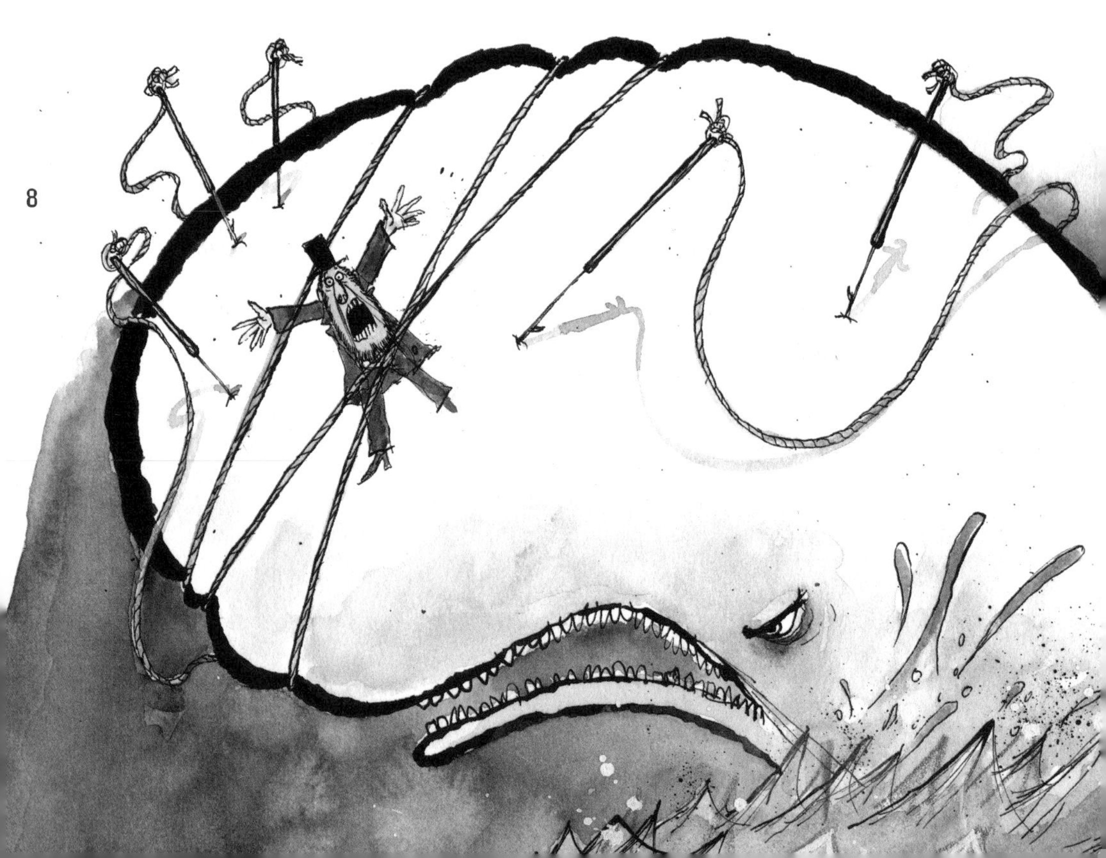

it's off to Nantucket for more clam chowder. Finally they set sail for three long and boring years at sea. Drive 'em out! Man the capstan! Stow the chowder! Then CAPTAIN AHAB appears on deck. He's handicapped. Only has one leg. It seems this big fish got the other one. He yells at his crew, "FIND ME THAT FISH, THE ONE THEY CALL MOBY DICK!" That's the one that's big and white and mean. And so the Pequod sails around Cape Horn. Ahab paces the deck. He yells at every passing ship, "HAVE YOU SEEN THE GREAT WHITE?" Next it's off to the Pacific. Ahab keeps pacing the deck as the ship sails on and on and on and on through hundreds of pages of painfully bad and pathetic paragraphs. "Have you seen the great white?" And another year goes by and then the lookout yells, "THAR SHE BLOWS!" It's big, it's white, it's mean, it's MOBY DICK! They all hop into the dinghies and they row for days, but Moby gets away. Then a typhoon hits. The sail gets ripped to shreds, and they all get wet. Then the lookout yells, "Thar she blows!" again. Back into the dinghies. This time they harpoon the heck outta Moby, which really gets him mad, so Moby munches a few men, bashes a few boats, punches the Pequod, GIVES AHAB A RIDE, and everybody dies but the fish and Ish.

GONE WITH THE WIND

GONE WITH THE WIND is the epic love story that chronicles the fall of the old South. This great book stars Clark Gable and Vivian Leigh and is the winner of ten Academy Awards. Here now is GONE WITH THE WIND.

SCARLETT O'HARA LOVES ASHLEY WILKES, but Ashley decides to marry Miss Melanie, which is announced at a party where Scarlett meets Rhett Butler, but SHE MARRIES CHARLES HAMILTON instead, who goes to war and dies along with just about everybody else except for Ashley, who comes to Atlanta on leave and then leaves while Atlanta burns and SCARLETT DELIVERS MELANIE'S BABY because Mammy isn't around to do it, and they all return to Tara. Scarlett's mother has typhoid and dies and the father has gone crazy and

Mammy has gone to ruin and EVERYBODY HAS TO PICK COTTON because they're poor now. Then SCARLETT KILLS A YANKEE while Ashley is taken prisoner, and he's released and returns to Tara because the war is over now, but they need three hundred dollars for taxes, so Mr. O'Hara chases the tax collector on his horse and dies, and Scarlett can't get the money from Rhett, so "FIDDLEDEEDEE." Scarlett tells Frank Kennedy that her sister's too ill and marry somebody else, and Scarlett marries him and GETS THE MONEY and also starts a successful lumber business with Ashley only to get mugged one day to have the guys go to avenge her which is when FRANK GETS KILLED AND DIES. That leaves Scarlett a widow again, so RHETT CAN FINALLY MARRY HER and take her to New Orleans for a honeymoon where Scarlett has a bad dream, forcing them to return to Tara where Scarlett gives birth to girl named Bonnie even though she still loves Ashley. Mammy yells at her some more and Rhett gets drunk and wants a divorce, but he takes Bonnie to London instead where *she* has a bad dream forcing *them* to return to Tara. BONNIE JUMPS ON HER HORSE AND DIES, and Melanie comes over to help but she's pregnant and dies. ASHLEY SAYS HE ALWAYS LOVED MELANIE NOT SCARLETT, so Scarlett decides she really does love Rhett after all, and Scarlett returns to Tara where Rhett says to her as he leaves her for good, "FRANKLY MY DEAR, I DON'T GIVE A DAMN," which makes Scarlett say, "Fiddledeedee, tomorrow is another day."

WANTED!
REWARD!

THE ADVENTURES OF ROBIN HOOD

Tales of ROBIN HOOD date back to fifteenth century England. Few stories have created more colorful a hero who, with his band of Merry Men, has captured the hearts of young and old alike. THE ADVENTURES OF ROBIN HOOD has earned a unique distinction in literature. It is the one story that everyone knows but no one has read.

Once upon a time in a place called SHERWOOD FOREST, there lived a famous outlaw named Robin Hood who wore tight GREEN TIGHTS and who stole from the rich and gave to the poor. One day Robin runs into a big guy named LITTLE JOHN. They hit each other with stout staffs, Ooo! Ah! Ow! And then Little John joins The Merry Men and puts on some green tights, too. Next, our sharpshooter from Sherwood steals a mutton joint from FRIAR TUCK and pushes him into the river. Then, everybody laughs. They're not called Merry Men for nothing. Back at Nottingham Castle THE EVIL SHERIFF SIGNS A DEATH WARRANT for our fearless hero in green, but nobody can catch Robin so the sheriff comes up with a plan: "LET'S HAVE A BOW AND ARROW CONTEST AND GET THAT GREEN GUY!" So our able archer arrives in disguise. Robin shoots his arrow, wins the golden arrow, and goes straight to jail. MAID MARIAN, who's got a thing for guys in green tights, helps Robin escape, the Merry Men shoot lots of arrows, and everybody rides horses back to Sherwood. Meanwhile back at the castle, THE SHERIFF OF NOTTINGHAM THROWS MAID MARIAN IN JAIL but wait—*do do-do do*—it's Robin Hood to the rescue! Robin runs into King Richard the Lionhearted who's on his way to the castle, too, so they all storm the castle, shoot all their arrows, and EVERYBODY GETS WHAT THEY WANT: Robin gets Marian, Marian gets Robin, Richard gets his throne back, and Robin Hood gets to hang up the green tights for good.

320·K

THE GRAPES OF WRATH

John Steinbeck's THE GRAPES OF WRATH is the story of the Joad family's eternal hopes and hardships. Set against the time of the Great Depression, Steinbeck's vivid imagery captures the courage, the dreams, the filth of the migrant worker.

TOM JOAD MAKES PAROLE, hitches a ride home, and runs into JIM CASEY and an Okie named MULEY GRAVES who babbles on and on about caterpillar tractors. Next day Tom and Jim go to UNCLE JOHN JOAD'S and it's a jolly Joad family indeed that greets Tom Joad at Uncle John Joad's. THE JOADS ARE JAZZED! They're going to CAL-I-FOR-NI-AY to work, for money, for food, to eat. So they sell everything they own for a lousy EIGHTEEN BUCKS and head out West.

Along the way on Route 66 the Joad's dog is run over, GRANDPA JOAD TURNS PURPLE AND DIES, the Joad jalopy breaks down, a camp official calls Tom a bum, and an Arizona border guard hassles the Joads. Ma Joad's worried about how much salt pork is left and then GRANDMA JOAD DIES as they cross the desert! BOY, ARE THESE JOADS JINXED. Finally they get to California where Tom trips up a deputy and Jim kicks the deputy in the neck! Tom goes to hide, Jim goes to jail, UNCLE JOHN GOES TO GET DRUNK.

With only ten potatoes left, the Joads have to hit the road again. Finally they stop to pick a few peaches for a nickel a box. Things are looking up! But then a cop smacks Jim Casey on the head and kills him so Tom turns around and kills *him*. So TOM JOAD LEAVES FOR GOOD and the Joads move into a dusty, dirty boxcar with the WAINWRIGHTS. Everybody picks a little cotton, but then the rain starts up and things go from bad to worse. Rose of Sharon gives birth to a dead baby and the Joads move into a barn.

So now the Joads have no money, no home, no car, no food, no work. The only thing they have is a family: A FAMILY OF JOADS. They have Pa Joad, Ma Joad, Uncle John Joad, Noah Joad, Al Joad, Sharon Joad, Ruthie Joad, Winfield Joad, and the newest Joad, wife of Al Joad, Agnes Joad. And that's A LOAD OF JOADS.

ROMEO & JULIET

ROMEO AND JULIET **is one of William Shakespeare's earliest dramatic works. For over three hundred years this tragic love story has delighted audiences around the world. It is with great pleasure that we now present** ROMEO AND JULIET.

Act I, scene 1:

It's another family feud in Verona. The CAPULETS, the villians; the MONTAGUES, the fools. Villians, fools, ooo, eee, oooahah.

Act I, scene 5:

Enter ROMEO, a hopelessly romantic 16-year-old kid who's trying to LOSE HIS VIRGINITY. Nothing much is happening when suddenly there she is—the delightful, the delicious, THE DELECTABLE JULIET. She's only 13, but who's counting? Not Romeo. So he says to her, "DEAR MAIDEN, MY LIPS, TWO BLUSHING PILGRIMS, READY STAND." They kiss and fall madly in love.

Act II, scene 2:

The famous balcony scene. Juliet's on the balcony. Romeo's in a bush. "Oh Romeo, Romeo, WHEREFORE ART THOU ROMEO?" They kiss a lot and the next thing you know they're married. That's it for the love story part. Now it's TIME FOR THE TRAGEDY.

Act III, scenes 1, 2, and 3:

TYBALT, the real macho type, kills some minor character named MERCUTIO. Then Romeo says, "Draw thy sword." They fight. Romeo wins, but ROMEO IS BANISHED from Verona anyway.

Act IV, scenes 1, 2, 3, 4, and 5:

Juliet's old man tells her to marry the goody-goody PARIS but she doesn't want to, so the fat friar makes Juliet a really STIFF DRINK, which makes it seem like JULIET'S DEAD but she really isn't. So the wedding is cancelled and they have a funeral for Juliet instead.

Act V, scenes 1, 2, and 3:

Romeo hears that Juliet's dead, but she really isn't. He TAKES THE POISON and says something that makes absolutely no sense at all: "Thou desperate pilot now at once run on the dashing rocks thy sea-sick weary bark." Then JULIET WAKES UP, but she thinks Romeo's

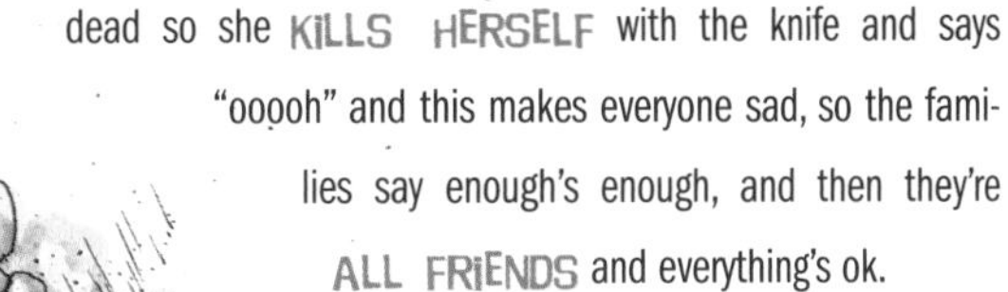

dead so she KILLS HERSELF with the knife and says "ooooh" and this makes everyone sad, so the families say enough's enough, and then they're ALL FRIENDS and everything's ok.

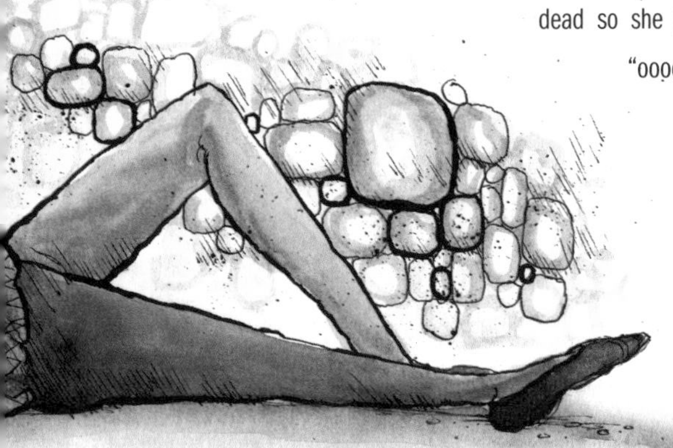

POP!
POP!
POP!
POP!

THE GREAT GATSBY

THE GREAT GATSBY **is the brilliant and strongly symbolic work of F. Scott Fitzgerald. In this great work of art, F. eloquently depicts the opulent lifestyle of upper class America during the roaring '20s. How great is** THE GREAT GATSBY**? Judge for yourself.**

DAISY AND HER HUSBAND TOM, who are both very rich, invite Daisy's cousin NICK, who's not so rich, over to East Egg and EVERYONE HAS A DRINK. The next day Tom is tired of counting his money, so Tom and Nick drive to GEORGE'S GARAGE to pick up George's wife MYRTLE (who is also Tom's mistress) so they can all go to New York for A PARTY. But Tom gets in a fight with Myrtle, Myrtle steps out of line, Tom breaks her nose, EVERYBODY HAS A DRINK. Then GATSBY, the racketeering romantic with a sensational smile who has amassed amazing amounts of cash in the hopes of winning back his darling Daisy, says, "OLD SPORT, LET'S HAVE SOME DRINKS AT MY PLACE." Next, Nick arranges a meeting between Daisy and Gatsby. Daisy arrives in a white car. She wears a white dress. She sees all the white flowers. She sees Gatsby who's wearing white. She's overcome.

She says, "White, my favorite color. LET'S HAVE A DRINK." Before

you know it, Daisy and Gatsby are spending many lazy, hung-over afternoons together. Next, it's time for another mindless dinner party. Everyone is rich, everyone is bored, so they drive to NEW YORK. Tom drives Gatsby's car, Gatsby drives Tom's car, Tom grabs a bottle of whiskey, and they go to the Plaza Hotel. THEY HAVE SOME DRINKS. Gatsby calls everyone "OLD SPORT." The whole gang gets BLITZED. On the way home, Daisy drives Gatsby's car. DAISY DOES 101 OVER MYRTLE. George wants revenge, so George gets out his GUN. He walks around all night looking for the car that mashed Myrtle. George walks back to West Egg, finds the car at Gatsby's big white house, walks up the big white stairs, sees Gatsby in the big, white pool, and he PULLS THE TRIGGER. And that's the very last for Mr. Jay Gatsby.

STELLA!!

A STREETCAR NAMED DESIRE

The winner of both the Pulitzer Prize and the Drama Critics Circle Award, A STREETCAR NAMED DESIRE is a portrait of Blanche DuBois, a beautiful woman who lives in conflict between a world of fantasy and tragedy. In this steamy drama, Tennessee Williams brings his characters and his audience to the melting point of passion and desire.

Scenes 1 and 2:

Hot summer night, NEW ORLEANS, the Kowalski apartment. Blanche DuBois arrives at her sister Stella's, has a few whiskeys, calls her sister "PRECIOUS LAMB," and says the family estate BELL REVE is sold. Then Blanche takes a BATH.

Scene 3:

Late that night, still hot. STANLEY, STEVE, MITCH, AND PABLO are playing poker. Blanche heads straight for the TUB, but she meets Mitch and they make small talk instead. They hang up a CHINESE

PAPER LANTERN, and Blanche turns on the radio. "SHUT THAT UP!" Stanley turns the radio off, Stella complains, Stanley turns Stella off, then Stanley takes a shower so he can go outside soaking wet in his ripped t-shirt and say "STELLA!"

Scene 4, 5, and 6:

Blanche knocks down a few SPIKED COKES and goes on a date with Mitch.

Scenes 7 and 8:

Four months later: STILL HOT. Blanche is back in the TUB. It's her birthday, so Stanley gives Blanche a ONE WAY BUS TICKET out of New Orleans. Everyone has a few pork chops, and Stanley clears the table.

Scene 9:

Later that night: even HOTTER. Blanche is boozing it up when Mitch confronts her with her PITIFUL PAST. Then Mitch turns on the lights. "No, no, not with that MESS OF MASCARA!"

Scene 10:

Same hot room. Blanche tells Stanley she's going on a CARIBBEAN CRUISE. Stanley rapes Blanche.

Scene 11:

A few weeks later: still hot. The guys play more poker and STELLA HAS A BABY. Then the doctor appears at the door, and Blanche says, "Whoever you are, I HAVE ALWAYS DEPENDED ON THE KINDNESS OF STRANGERS." Then they take Blanche away and it's not to the Caribbean.

EAT
ME!

ALICE IN WONDERLAND

ALICE IN WONDERLAND is Lewis Carroll's delightful children's story that is more than just a whimsical tale of a young girl's adventures. It is also a complex work of literature that satirizes the values of Victorian life. Inspired by Carroll's life-long fascination with ten-year-old girls, this enchanting fantasy has been a favorite of children and adults alike for over one hundred years.

Alice is bored because her sister is reading a book when, all of a sudden, a WHITE RABBIT wearing a vest runs by mumbling something about being late. Not being able to mind her own business, Alice follows the rabbit into A HOLE and falls down and down, landing with a thud. Alice finds a bottle that says "DRINK ME," so she drinks it and gets very, very SMALL. She finds a cake that says "EAT ME," so she eats it and gets very, very tall. "CURIOUSER AND CURIOUSER!" cries Alice, which isn't good English but it gets the point across. Then Alice begins to shrink again and falls into a pool of her own tears along with a mouse, a duck, a Dodo, a lawyer, and an eaglet. After another grueling round of "DRINK ME, EAT ME," Alice runs into the woods where she meets a BLUE CATERPILLAR sitting on a mushroom puffing on a HOOKAH. "Alice, baby, what's happening, mellow out, this is WONDERLAND." So Alice chomps on some MUSHROOMS and the Duchess sneezes because there's too much pepper in the soup. The CHESHIRE CAT keeps grinning and the world's ugliest baby turns into a squirming pig. Then it's time for tea. The MAD HATTER, the MARCH HARE, and the sleepy DORMOUSE talk in stupid riddles so Alice finds more stimulating conversation in a GARDEN OF TALKING FLOWERS. Next the QUEEN OF HEARTS plays croquet with flamingo mallets and hedgehog balls, and then Alice takes the stand in the TRIAL OF THE MISSING TARTS. Alice's testimony so angers the queen that she shouts, "OFF WITH HER HEAD!" which is Alice's cue to wake up and face the facts. It was all just a dream and a good thing too for Alice knew nothing of tarts and even less of torts.

OLIVER TWIST

Charles Dicken's OLIVER TWIST is the story of a young boy's harsh but exciting adventures in a city of cruel masters, cunning thieves, and rewarding friendships. In this great novel, Dickens exposes the darkness of crime and reveals the ultimate triumph of love. A work of prestigious length, it is no surprise Dickens was paid by the word.

A young woman who was about to die in a workhouse leaves a newborn baby with a bully named BUMBLE who tags the toddler OLIVER TWIST. Oliver scarfs down some porridge for nine years in an orphanage and when he says, "PLEASE SIR, SOME MORE," Oliver is kicked out. So he hitches a ride to LONDON where he bumps into the ARTFUL DODGER, a young pickpocket who brings him to FAGIN, the miserly master of the gang of juvenile delinquents who steal snuffboxes and hankies. Oliver then gets caught and rescued by BROWNLOW, who raises Oliver because Oliver just *happens* to look like some lady in a portrait. Then NANCY, who lives with nasty BILL SIKES, who works with Fagin, who eats little boys for breakfast, robs a house with Oliver, and OLIVER'S SHOT and then nursed back to health by MRS. MAYLIE and her adopted daughter ROSE (who just *happen* to be the same people who live in the same house that Oliver tried to rob). Then Fagin and a guy with a scar named MONKS track Oliver down, but NANCY GETS COLD FEET and warns Rose (whose name she just *happened* to hear Monks mention to Fagin), so ROSE TAKES OLIVER BACK TO BROWNLOW. But Sikes just *happens* to overhear Nancy's conversation with Rose, which incites Sikes to kill Nancy, but Brownlow finds Monks anyway, who just *happens* to be Oliver's half brother and tells Brownlow of his plans to keep all of their FATHER'S INHERITANCE. But Oliver's mother just *happened* to have a little sister who just *happened* to be none other than Rose, who's Oliver's aunt. Plus Brownlow just *happened* to be Oliver's father's BEST FRIEND, which means absolutely nothing to Sikes and Fagin, who get SNUFFED OUT anyway. But for Oliver, it means he just *happens* to be related to absolutely everyone else in the book, which just *happens* to be one BIG COINCIDENCE.

THE ODYSSEY

THE ODYSSEY is the legendary epic tale composed by the blind poet Homer. The tale of Odysseus was first presented in pre-literate Greece by professional storytellers. So imagine, if you will, that the year is 500 B.C., that you are somewhere in Greece, and you don't know how to read.

After the TROJAN WAR, it was ten years before Odysseus returns home to Greece where his wife PENELOPE WAS WAITING, weaving, and fending off lots of muscle-bound Hercules-types. Where was Odysseus all this time? EATING BAKLAVA WITH THE BEAUTIFUL NYMPH CALYPSO on her Mediterranean island for eight years. That's how badly he wanted to get home.

Finally, Odysseus hits the open sea only to have good old POSEIDON WRECK HIS SHIP. But Odysseus is rescued and tells his story. And if there's one thing Odysseus can do, it's talk. So here's what happens: Odysseus and his men LEAVE TROY VICTORIOUS, but they're blown to the LAND OF THE LOTUS EATERS and sack out for a while, while in the Lotus position. At the next port of call, the ONE-EYED CYCLOPS eats two of his men for dinner and two more for breakfast before they escape to the EDGE OF THE WORLD. That's where all the dead people live. They reminisce about old dead friends, drink a little blood. Then they sail past the ISLAND OF THE SIRENS with their seductive song. AAAAAAH! Luckily, they all had WAX IN THEIR EARS so no one heard a thing. Then the SIX-HEADED MONSTER, SCYLLA, chomps down six more of the crew before the rest of the guys say "VWAT THE HELL," and they shish kabob some SACRED COWS belonging to HYPERION, THE SUN GOD. The gods get angry again and they kill everyone else except for our hero, who somehow manages to get home. Then with the help of ATHENA, GODDESS OF WISDOM AND ARTS AND CRAFTS, Odysseus kills just about everyone. Then he takes a break: he makes love to his wife, visits his dad, has some souvlaki for lunch. Then he starts killing again, but this time ZEUS, KING OF THE GODS, intervenes: "NAUGHT IN OUGHT, ODYSSEUS!" And when Zeus talks, everyone listens.